LIGHT BULBS
and
LOLLYPOPS

Living
~~Looking~~ on the Bright Side of Life

BRONWYN HALLOT

Copyright © 2024 Bronwyn Hallot. All rights reserved.

All rights reserved. This book may not be copied or reprinted for commercial gain or profit. The use of short quotations or occasional page copying for personal, or group study is permitted and encouraged. Unless otherwise identified, Scripture quotations are from The Passion Translation and the Amplified Bible.

ISBN: 979-8-89316-088-8 (paperback)
ISBN: 979-8-89316-089-5 (ebook)

This book is dedicated to my husband. Without his courage, unconditional love and unwavering support, much of this book would not have been written.

This book is dedicated to my husband, without whom...

Foreword

We have had the privilege of journeying with Bronwyn over the last five years through School of Faith and most recently as one of the leaders of Te Puna Wai Church Movement. She carries a strong mantle to see strongholds broken in the lives of people, and them being restored to fullness and living empowered lives.

There is a growing need for people to be authentic. At the writing of this foreword, the most looked up word in the Merriam-Webster's Word of the Year for 2023 is 'authentic—the term for something we're thinking about, writing about, aspiring to, and judging more than ever'. In her latest book, Light Bulbs and Lollipops – Living on the Bright Side of Life, Bronwyn has generously shared her life stories through being vulnerable, transparent and giving us a true living testimony of an authentic believer. She has lived experience of what it is to go through pain, loss, tragedy and deep betrayal.

Bronwyn provides practical insights and scripture to support anyone towards living a brighter life. Her tips and strategies come from her own victories. She has also drawn inspiration from leading experts such as Mark Virkler, Chris Gore and the writings of Fernando Pessoa.

We all have choices. Whether we have disappointment, discouragement or feel powerless to overcome desperate situations. Bronwyn urges us to consider that we have a choice to change the narrative and to choose to "be an encouragement, not take offence, to forgive, to see the gold in others", and to find a way forward.

Bronwyn is a living testimony of someone who walks on the bright side of life. As you read this book, you will learn to walk in a greater measure of breakthrough in your own life, that will position you to help others, in the same way that Bronwyn is doing by writing and releasing this book.

Bronwyn's heart is that we may all walk in peace and love as we come to know the person of Peace and Love, who is Jesus Christ. As you read this book, we encourage you to grab your journal and a pen and start the journey towards living on the bright side of life, as Bronwyn leads you there with her insights.

Selwyn and Kelly Bennett
School of Faith NZ, Captains
Senior Leaders – Te Puna Wai Church

Contents

Foreword v
Introduction xi

Positive Thinking

Chapter 1:   Power up the Positive, Park the Negative 1
Chapter 2:   Speak Life, not Death 9
Chapter 3:   From Disappointment to Encouragement 15
Chapter 4:   Choosing Joy 23

Weathering the Storm

Chapter 5:   Finding Rest in a Busy World 29
Chapter 6:   Staying in Rest while the Storm is Raging 35
Chapter 7:   Finding Peace in the Storm 41
Chapter 8:   Warring Through Rest 47

Being an Overcomer

Chapter 9:   Being an Overcomer: From Fear to Faith 53
Chapter 10: Keeping Hearts of Hope in Difficult Times 59

Chapter 11: The Power of His Love; Learning to Overcome
   Through Love 65
Chapter 12: Forgiving the Unforgivable 71
Chapter 13: Living Free 81

Conclusion 89
Acknowledgements 91
Author Biography 93

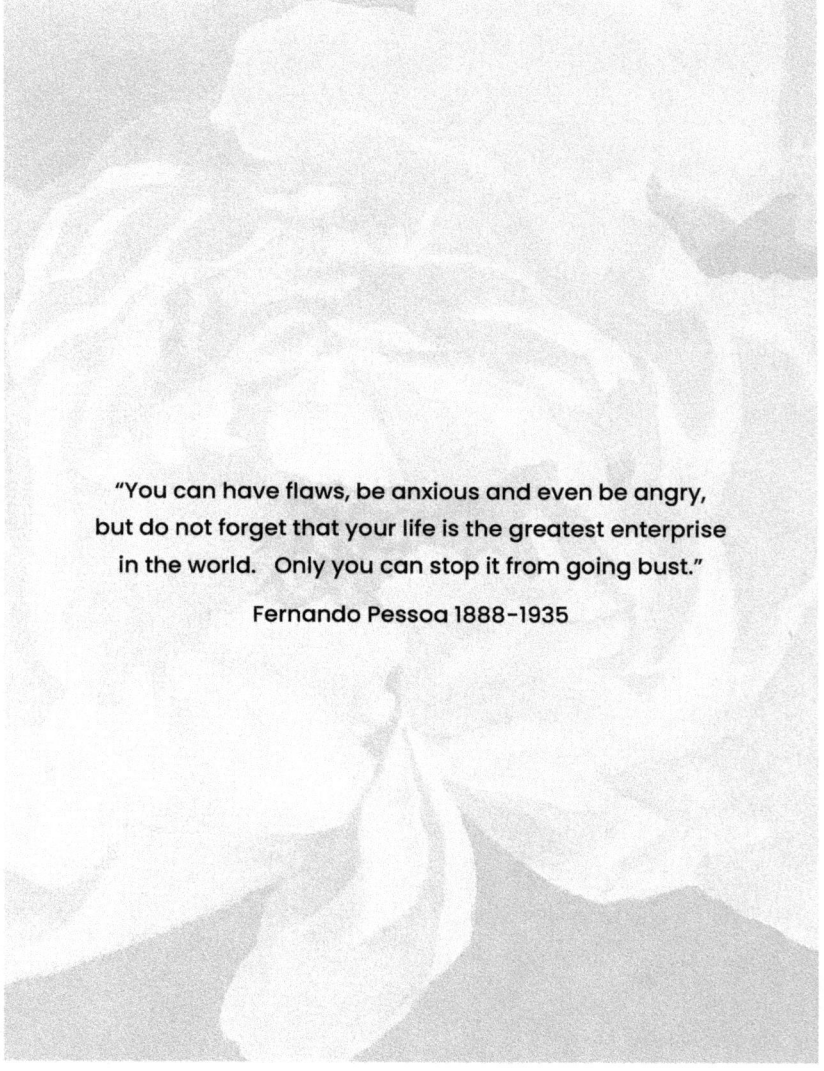

"You can have flaws, be anxious and even be angry, but do not forget that your life is the greatest enterprise in the world. Only you can stop it from going bust."

Fernando Pessoa 1888-1935

INTRODUCTION

Introduction

How do we remain positive in a world where negative news is everywhere? It seems as if every headline is designed to highlight the darker aspects of life. Even if a story is positive, there is a tendency to dig up a negative aspect to focus on. We live in an age of character assassination, criticism and negativity. What is our position, our place, and how do we navigate our way through it all?

In this book you will discover some tips and keys to make choices that will help change the environment around you, through how you think, speak and respond. Many people believe that we cannot change the environment because life just happens. It is true that there can be circumstances which affect us through no fault of our own. However, we always have a choice about how we process, receive and act upon what happens around us.

When our three children were young, our world was tipped upside down in a matter of weeks. We no longer had our own home, could not afford to rent one and the children's dad was living far away from us. The trauma and emotions surrounding that time in our lives cannot be underestimated. There were days when I wanted to pull the covers up over my head and shut out the world. However, there were three young people relying on me to be the adult, to be the strength they needed to give them the courage to get out and face the world. The circumstances could not be changed, nevertheless I could make a choice to get out of that bed, be loving and strong for my children, hold my chin up, put my shoulders back and face the world. Thank God I did.

This challenging experience, among others in my life, taught me valuable lessons in creating a positive environment for myself and those around me. It became a journey of encouragement, forgiveness, and finding the gold in others during times of adversity.

In these pages it is my hope that you too will find a lifeline, a way forward to making your own life more positive, joyful, encouraging and fulfilling. Maybe receive some inner healing, should that be necessary. As you embark upon this journey, a few words of reflection taken from an excerpt by Portuguese poet Fernando Pessoa.

Many are those who appreciate you, admire you and love you. You don't know, but there are people for whom you are special. I want you to remember that happiness is not having a sky without storms, a road without accidents, work without fatigue, relationships without disappointments. To be happy is finding strength in forgiveness, hope in battles, security in the stage of fear, love in discord. It's like walking through deserts outside of self but being able to find an oasis deep within your soul. It is to thank God for every morning, for the miracle of life. It is to have maturity to be able to say, "I made mistakes." Having the courage to say, "Forgive me." It is to have the sensitivity to say, "I need you". It is having the ability to say, "I love you." May your life become a garden of opportunities for happiness. That in spring may it be a lover of joy. In winter a lover of wisdom. And then when you make a mistake, start all over again. For only then will you be in love with life.

As you read, have a pen and paper or a journal handy so you can reflect, ask or answer questions, or set yourself some life changing goals. Regardless of what you are going through right now, or your life story to this point, you too can make changes as to how you view your world. May lightbulb moments brighten up your day. May lollipops, laughter, joy infused fun be part of this journey also, to help you live on the bright side of life.

> For with the heart, one believes and is justified and with the mouth one confesses and is saved.
>
> Romans 10:10

POWER UP THE POSITIVE, PARK THE NEGATIVE

Chapter 1
POWER UP THE POSITIVE, PARK THE NEGATIVE

What brings positivity into your life? Is it the weather, uplifting music, encouraging words, the company of loved ones, or perhaps your faith? On the flip side, what triggers negativity for you? Is it unexpected overwhelming situations, social media comments, workplace irritations, or exposure to distressing news?

In our post Covid world, negativity seems more pervasive than ever. It appears that we are under a constant stream of information through social media, news sites, and video clips. Our exposure to dramatic global events is at a frequency our ancestors never experienced. Unlike them, we live in an era of instant information, where news is not solely delivered by reputable channels but also by social media and various online platforms. How is this constant stream of news affecting our thoughts, our attitudes and behaviours and ultimately our overall sense of well being?

How truthful is it? All news is factual from the perspective of the person writing or reporting it. There are, after all, two sides to every story. An illustration of this I noticed in a newspaper article recently showed two photos of Prince William. The one above shows Prince William in an animated conversation with a member of the public in a seemingly large crowd lining the streets to see him. His hand and middle finger held aloft. To the reader it looks like he is giving the 'bird', the 'finger', to someone in the crowd. This seems very out of character and a bit strange. However, the second photo below, shows the exact same moment taken by a photographer on the other side of Prince William. The second photo shows him holding up his hand which clearly has three fingers, not one, visible. If we had only been privy to the first photograph, we would be thinking that Prince William was being incredibly rude to a member of the public. We would not have known any different, because that would have been the only side of the news that we were shown. Thankfully having two sides to the story, we were able to see that the first photo was extremely misleading.

> **Keep your thoughts fixed on whatever is true, whatever is honourable, whatever is commendable, if there is any excellence, if there is anything worthy of praise. Think about these things.**
> **Philippians 4:8**

This scripture from Paul to the Phillipians gives a remedy, a solution and insight into how we can find a better way to generate a more positive environment to live in.

Where are our eyes and ears focussing? What we spend most of our time in, will influence how we think and feel. Fear can infiltrate our thinking so subtly. We can't make the news of the world go away, but we can make choices about what and how much we hear and see. Choosing to limit news is really helpful in creating a more positive environment. Just because it is there, do we need to view it? It was a choice I made some time ago to desist from viewing the evening news on television. No longer was I prepared to tune into the constant barrage of relatively minor news events being crafted into something much bigger. The interviewing of many 'specialists' or 'authorities' to speak on 'what might happen if', blurs the facts and the possible scenario now becomes the focus. Have you ever noticed how, nine times out of ten, these 'what if' situations never arise? However, in the process, unconsciously, people are being filled with doubt and fear to ponder on.

Am I suggesting we shouldn't keep in touch with what is happening around the world? No, it is important to be informed. My preferred source of news comes from a reputable radio news channel each morning. If it starts to go down the rabbit hole of negative investigations, the off button works splendidly.

What about social media's influence on our sense of well being? Can it too influence negativity? Do we find this is an area that brings out positive and heartwarming interactions? Or do we come away from posts on social media feeling irritated and annoyed? Do we feel like dumping our opinion in the chat and letting them have it? If we responded that social media is a place of great positivity for us, that is wonderful. However, if we find that the time we are spending on social media is causing irritation, frustration and an angry response arising, maybe it is time to stop and critically consider where we are spending our time and what we are spending our time viewing?

Do you know about algorithms? Seriously, I don't understand all the science behind it, but I know enough to know that they are designed to pick up on what sites we are searching and to link us with similar sites of interest. An example of this might be. We find ourselves drawn to exploring creative ideas for our passion of upcycling secondhand clothing. Our digital journey leads us to diverse online platforms dedicated to these passions. Each search leaves a mark whereby our computer opens up to a cascade of related content, fostering a positive environment. However, conversely, let's look at a scenario where this can trigger a negative outcome. Maybe we harbour discontent with a political party or current government? In our quest for understanding, we view official government policies and articles, then videos from individuals who too are harbouring deep scepticism towards the authorities. As we immerse ourselves in their narratives, a continuous stream of negative content about the government floods our screens and impacts our thinking. This amplifies our dissatisfaction, creating a feedback of negativity. The subtle shift occurs as our exposure to only negative viewpoints leaves us with a skewed perspective generating a far from positive platform to land on.

Still on the subject of what we spend our time viewing, where we set our eyes and how it can affect our environment in either negative or positive ways, is how we view our friend's information posted on social media. How do we respond to viewpoints that we don't align to? That might even raise an angry or irrational response? We are not always going to agree with what our friends post. However, they are entitled to their opinions and interests that they are passionate about. If it does not line up with ours and we struggle to read what they are posting, we can choose to remove ourselves from the friendship group. We do not have to attack them personally or attack their posts. If we can position ourselves in a place of love, then we are less likely to get into a negative spiral of attack and instead, agree to disagree on what we think. In this way we uphold a positive outcome.

Another sphere of influence that can affect how positive or negative we feel daily can be the conversations that take place around us and the part we play in them. It really is a blessing if we are surrounded by friends, family and work colleagues who have a positive outlook, but we all know that often our workplace can have a few colleagues who struggle to see the positive in their circumstances. Our workplace environment can be a place where critical conversations take place behind someone's back. If we are not clear about how we want to behave or what we value, this kind of environment can easily suck us in.

In my own home, family and friendship environment, we see the positive qualities in each other and offer encouragement. However, my professional experience has exposed me to environments where a culture of criticism and backbiting have undermined others. There was a time when I found myself entangled in such negativity, contributing to disparaging discussions. One day, I decided to break free from this cycle , declaring to myself, 'This ends today. I refuse to live my life this way at work when it is not how I live at home.' The true test of this commitment came early one morning when faced with a negative conversation. I immediately informed my colleague, 'I won't participate in this conversation. It's not who I am outside of work and I won't engage in tearing others down within the workplace. I prefer to discover the positive aspects in people, so let's focus on that.'

Many opportunities will present themselves to be around people who frustrate us, let us down, or fail to find positivity. However, it is crucial to remain true to our values. If we try to look for the positive angle, find a little something to encourage and build up, rather than tearing down, we can make a difference. Not only to our own sense of feeling positive, but hopefully, for people around us. At the very least, if we genuinely are having trouble finding something positive to say, then we can stay silent. We don't have to join in.

How does this make our environment more positive? Creating a positive environment is essential. In a critical, backbiting setting, the atmosphere is perpetually unpleasant knowing that the conversations about us will occur as soon as we leave the room. Speaking negatively behind others' backs leaves a bitter aftertaste, offering no benefits for a personal or collective uplifting atmosphere. Making a difference starts with a conscious choice to foster positivity and encouragement.

Do not let any unwholesome talk come out of your mouths, but only what is helpful for building others up according to their needs, that it may benefit those who listen.
Ephesians 4:29

In your journal, reflect on your own surroundings, whether in the workplace or among friends. Regarding habits around news, social media and general internet usage, consider how you can contribute to a positive environment that builds up rather than tears down.

If you already practise great strategies to remain positive, even in the midst of negativity around you, reflect and write down the ways you do that. Celebrate and give thanks.

He speaks into existence, that which is not, as though it were.

Romans 4:17

SPEAK LIFE NOT DEATH

Chapter 2
SPEAK LIFE, NOT DEATH

> Life and death are in the power of the tongue.
> Proverbs 18:21

We have heard "Sticks and stones can break my bones, but names will never hurt me." Never was there a more untrue statement. As a teacher for most of my life teaching children from ages five to 18 across my career, there were often times spent on helping young people cope with what the tongue had unleashed. We can recover very satisfactorily, usually, from a broken bone. However, the depth of the wounds that are left from careless words lashed out in anger, jealousy, disappointment or whatever the cause, can last a lifetime.

Many people who suffer from conditions such as eating disorders, anxiety, depression, suicidal thoughts and the like, can be as a result from words that have been spoken over them. Even comments that are claimed to be spoken in jest, leave their mark. Words are powerful. They can link and form chains that bind our thinking about ourselves.

What comes out of our mouths brings life or death. Dr Masaru Emoto, the Japanese scientist who revolutionised the idea that our thoughts and intentions impact the physical realm, is one of the most important water researchers the world has known. For over 20 years until he passed away in 2014, he studied the scientific evidence of how the molecular structure in water transforms when it is exposed to human words, thoughts, sounds and intentions. Dr Masaru Emoto's water experiment found that water exposed to positive words and intentions formed beautiful, symmetrical crystalline structures when the water was frozen, while water exposed to negative words and intentions formed disorganised, asymmetrical structures. Water has a memory. (akwl.org) Considering that our bodies are made up of approximately 60% water, this is very interesting research.

> **Out of the heart the mouth speaks.**
> **Luke 6:45**

It has occurred to me, over the years, that we all have 'filters', some might call it 'lenses', by which we see and hear the world around us. Depending on the influences, positive or negative we have had directed towards us throughout our life, will determine how clear or clogged our filters are.

When my husband and I initially started dating, it became apparent that he often viewed himself through a negative filter, which sometimes extended to his perceptions of others. His default mode seemed defensive, as if he were constantly under attack. A simple illustration of this was when calling out to him from the kitchen, "Thank you for emptying the dishwasher." An appreciative, heartfelt response to a job well done was greeted with "I DID!". It seemed he interpreted my acknowledgement as sarcasm, perceiving an accusation rather than genuine praise.

At the time of writing, we have been married for 17 years during which time my husband has made significant strides in overcoming feelings of inadequacy rooted in a childhood marked by discouraging comments. Despite being deeply loved by his parents and sisters, he grappled with a persistent sense of falling short in his father's eyes. While this may seem like an unfounded perception, both of his sisters affirm that they witnessed moments of mistreatment and harsh words during his upbringing. It brings immense joy to say that in the latter years of his father's life, my husband and his dad cultivated a profoundly loving relationship. They addressed any misunderstandings and forgave past grievances, with his father expressing genuine pride in him.

Nevertheless, it has taken many years, in fact it is an ongoing journey, for my husband to clear negativity from his filter enabling him to accept compliments and encouragement with the love that was intended. A journey which demonstrates the profound impact of words and actions.

> Guard your heart above all else, for it
> determines the course of your life.
> Proverbs 4:2

The words we speak are an indicator of what is in our hearts. What comes out of our mouths during testing situations, when our guard is down? Entertaining some gossip? Justifying our mistake? Caught in a traffic jam or running late for an appointment? A colleague struggling to juggle the workload? The condition of our heart is demonstrated by how we respond. Delight at another's adversity, making excuses, anger, criticism and comparison? How do we change our heart to change the way we speak? How do we start bringing life into our conversations instead of speaking death through what we say?

One example of how bringing life into our words involves a conscious decision to abstain from certain words or activities such as whether to engage in gossip - those intricately detailed or embellished stories passed from one person to another.

I recall an incident from years ago when our children were young. A knock on the door revealed a neighbour, not a close friend but someone with whom we maintained friendly relations. Without waiting for an invitation, she launched into scandalous gossip about an unfamiliar person in the community. Politely, when the opportunity presented itself, through an intake of breath, I expressed my lack of knowledge about the individual and made it clear that it was not my concern. Surprisingly, she seemed taken aback by my disinterest. Excusing herself, she quickly proceeded across the road to share the gossip with another neighbour.

> Let love and faithfulness never leave you; bind them around your neck, write them on the tablet of your heart. Then you will win favour and a good name in the sight of God and man.
> Proverbs 3:3-4 NIV

We have all experienced moments we are not proud of. Some indiscretions can be discreetly swept under the carpet, without public witness. For others our misfortunes become painfully visible, either due to our actions or those within our close circles. We know what it feels like, or can imagine how it feels to be the subject of gossip. While some may be indifferent, for most of us, it is uncomfortable. Imagine if the tables were turned - if it were us or our family under the spotlight. Would we want our private matters dissected in hushed conversations, social media threads, or office discussions? We cannot control the actions of others but we can make the choice to halt gossip in us.

Some time ago my husband and I came to a consensus that if sad or surprising news has come to our attention about someone, we make it an opportunity to pray for that person or organisation. To speak truth and life over them for good. If we have not been privy to the information, then we have no business being involved in any conversation about them. In other words, it is not our business. We can however lift the situation in prayer, that it will work out for good.

Changing the condition of the heart to speak life giving words comes from the knowledge of knowing how loved we are. His love for us came before we chose to love Him. It is from this dwelling place of love that we can begin to consider others more deeply and lovingly. Being responsible for and owning our own actions instead of looking for excuses. Flipping a switch from anger at outward circumstances such as the traffic jam causing us to be late, to recognising there is nothing we can do to move the traffic any faster, agitation certainly won't do it, so commit to enjoying the slower moment. To the colleague who may not be getting through the workload as quickly or efficiently as their predecessor. Criticism won't help them improve, kind words of encouragement and an offer of help, certainly will.

> **Be kind and compassionate to one another, forgiving each other, just as Christ God forgave you.**
> **Ephesians 4:32 NIV**

Is being more positive in what you speak, an area that you would like to practise and develop? In your journal, take a moment to reflect on some possible choices you might make, to speak life more abundantly in the conversations and interactions around you.

FROM DISAPPOINTMENT TO ENCOURAGEMENT

Chapter 3
FROM DISAPPOINTMENT TO ENCOURAGEMENT

Closely connected with the impact of words that either bring life or inflict harm is the experience of finding ourselves in a place of disappointment and discouragement. Various factors, words being a contributor, can lead us to these destinations. What are the triggers that can bring discouragement for you? Take a moment to jot down those instances that can influence your emotional well-being.

Disappointment can often come through our setting very high expectations of a person or a situation, only to find that the picture in our mind is a far cry from the reality. While it is important that we set high expectations for ourselves, it is also important that these expectations are realistic and achievable. However, we must be very careful that we don't have an expectation of someone that we have not communicated to them. To have a picture and not communicate it, is highly likely to end in disappointment. No one else will have the same picture as you.

We can be our own source of disappointment too, through things we have done or said that did not line up with our values or expectations. Also, through goals we have set for ourselves that we didn't achieve as well as we had hoped. These can be reasons to feel disappointed. How do we move from disappointment to encouragement in these circumstances?

The most important thing is to be kind to ourselves. Firstly, acknowledge what we are disappointed about. Was there anything we could have done differently for a different outcome? Is there anything we need to do going forward to either fix, improve or gain a different outcome? If so, then put that plan into place. If not, forgive yourself and let it go.

We can alleviate some disappointment from our lives through clear communication, setting expectations for ourselves and others that are achievable and realistic. We can reduce disappointment with ourselves by being practical about what is possible going forward, to change the situation or as suggested earlier, be kind, forgive ourselves and move on.

Discouragement can slip into our lives very easily, if we let it. It can often come through being expectant for something that is taking a long time to come to pass. It could be the hope of healing, waiting for an operation, taking longer than you thought to recover from something, waiting for a promotion that was promised but has not come through. It can come from discouraging words from others, making you feel like you don't measure up, you aren't good enough or bright enough, which can feed into a negative self-belief.

What can we do if we feel discouraged, or feel like we don't measure up? There are things we can do. My greatest source of encouragement has come from what God says about me in his Word. When we know how He sees us, how much He treasures us, how unique and special we are and that we are fearfully and wonderfully made, we come to a point where it really doesn't matter what others say about us. His opinion is the only one that matters.

Below are some of those very special scriptures. There are so many more and I encourage you to seek them out, write them on notes and put them around your mirror, on your fridge or calendar, in your diary, wherever you are most likely to see them. Speak and declare them until you truly believe it about yourself. It is very hard to be discouraged when you are filled up with words of loving encouragement.

God says I am forever loved.

> So now I live with the confidence that there is nothing in the universe with the power to separate us from God's love. I'm convinced that His love will triumph over death, life's troubles, fallen angels, or dark rulers in the heavens. There is nothing in our present or future circumstances that can weaken His love.
> Romans 8:38-39

God says I am wonderfully made.

> For You formed my innermost parts; You knit me together in my mother's womb. I will give thanks and praise to You, for I am fearfully and wonderfully made.
> Psalm 139:13

God says I am healed.

> But He was wounded for our transgressions, He was crushed for our wickedness, our sin, our injustice, our wrongdoing; The punishment required for our well-being fell on Him, and by His stripes, wounds, we are healed.
> Isaiah 53:5

God says He makes me strong.

> The God who encircles me with strength
> and makes my way blameless.
> Psalm 18:32

God says I am forgiven.

> I remind you, dear children. Your sins have been
> permanently removed because of the power of His name.
> 1 John 2:12

God says I am adopted in God's family.

> For it was always in His perfect plan to adopt
> us as His delightful children, through our
> union with Jesus, the Anointed one.
> Ephesians 1:5

God says He makes me whole.

> And in Him you have been made complete.
> Colossians 2:10

God says He is always with me.

> Have I not commanded you? Be strong and
> courageous! Do not be terrified or dismayed, for
> the Lord your God is with you wherever you go.
> Joshua 1:9

God says because of Him I am hopeful.

> For I know the plans and thoughts that I have for you,
> says the Lord, plans for peace and well-being and
> not for disaster, to give you a future and a hope.
> Jeremiah 29:11
> (One of my favourite verses)

God says I was created with purpose.

> And who knows whether you have attained royalty
> for such a time as this and for this very purpose?
> Esther 4:14

God says I am victorious in Christ.

> But we thank God for giving us the victory as conquerors
> through our Lord Jesus, the Anointed One.
> 1 Corinthians 15:57

There are times when discouragement is not about, or from us, but from unfulfilled circumstances or unanswered prayer. Bill Johnson of Bethel Church, Redding California talks of being in a place of discouragement, especially if it has come about because of expectancy with God that has not yet eventuated. It might be a loved one who you have been praying for healing and they pass away. He says get alone with God and speak to him and say things like, "It looks like you lied, you don't lie but it sure looks like it." Stay there with Him in His Word, reading and spending time with Him, until you come out feeling encouraged.

In your journal write down areas in your life where you might be feeling some disappointment or discouragement. Write out some of the above scriptures that resonated with you, that you are going to start speaking over yourself.

Reflect and record some of the little things that you are thankful for. Celebrate them.

Now may God, the inspiration and fountain of hope fill you to overflowing with uncontainable joy and perfect peace as you trust in him.

Romans 15:13

CHOOSING JOY

Chapter 4
CHOOSING JOY

What are the elements that brighten your day and bring joy into your life? A beautiful sunny day, relaxing on holiday, a pay rise or new job opportunity, the satisfaction of delicious coffee or a delightful meal shared with friends, the simple joy of laughter with children, animals or during a captivating movie? Because you choose to be joyful? Take a moment to create a list of these sources of joy in your life.

Alternatively, it is important to recognise the factors or triggers that have the potential to rob you of your joy, bringing about a change in mood. What are the elements that tend to bring you down? Consider instances or circumstances that have done this. Compile a list of these joy robbers as a starting point for understanding and addressing sources of negativity in your life.

There are so many wonderful opportunities to be filled with joy. However, looking at your lists, is your joy only determined by your circumstances? Do we allow our circumstances and experiences to be the source of our joy, rather than being joyful within, regardless of our circumstances?

We have all encountered individuals in our workplaces, communities, and perhaps even within our families, who struggle to express positivity due to allowing external circumstances to rob them of joy. They often fall victim to self-fulfilling prophecies, consistently stating, 'That always happens to me', or 'That never happens to me.' Recognising whether we have been influenced by external factors is evident through our words and behaviours. How can we choose to be joyful, even in difficult circumstances?

> **Consider it pure joy, my brothers and sisters, whenever you face trials of many kinds, because you know that the testing of your faith produces perseverance.**
> **James 1:2**

If your joy is determined by your circumstances only, then how is that working for you? What happens when your joy triggers are not happening? The skies are grey, the coffee shop is closed, the jokes aren't funny? It is so easy to slide down that slippery slope into feeling out of sorts, not happy with the world. Placing all our joy on things and experiences rather than choosing to be joyful regardless of outward circumstances, means when these outside influences are, or are not happening, we are robbed of our joy.

A gloriously sunny day brings out the best in me. My energy levels increase, I feel so productive and upbeat. When the sun is warming my bones and the option of being outdoors in the garden, cycling or just enjoying the day is a possibility its effect is extremely uplifting. There are times, in the area where I live, when we can experience a lot of rain and gloomy, grey, cloudy days. To be honest, I have to catch myself from feeling disgruntled if that kind of weather persists.

My antidote is to choose joy. I cannot change the weather, but I can choose my mood, to delight in things other than the weather. When the sun does come out, that will be the icing on the cake, not the main event of my day.

How do we find sources of joy that are not determined from outside influences?

> These things I have spoken to you, that my joy
> may be in you, and that your joy may be full.
> 5 John 15:11

> Though you have not seen Him, you love Him; and
> even though you do not see Him now, you believe
> in Him and are filled with an inexpressible and
> glorious joy, for you are receiving the end result
> of your faith, the salvation of your souls.
> 1 Peter 1:8-9

"Okay", I hear you saying, "That is all very well. I don't have to be joyful all the time! Some days I just don't feel like it and surely that is okay?" Absolutely, it is okay not to have to feel joyful all the time. However, it is important that we recognise our flat or negative moods and are equipped to know how to generate our own joy. This way we won't stay camped there waiting for circumstances around us to change before feeling upbeat again. Avoiding being a prisoner to outward circumstances rather than choosing our own.

A powerful source of joy for me lies in recognising and embracing my identity in Him, understanding the depth of His love for me. My heart is full of joy in that knowledge. Gratitude for my husband, family, where we live, our friends, for employment amplifies this joy. It is really hard to be discouraged or sad when you have a heart full of thanksgiving. So now how can we put this into practise and change the atmosphere within us, to change the environment around us?

We can:

- Spend time meditating on the scriptures about joy
- Sing songs
- Listen to our favourite music
- Join someone else and sing
- Dance, praise and worship
- Pray
- Watch funny clips on Instagram
- Call a friend
- Help someone, taking our minds off ourselves
- Generate activities that we enjoy like cycling, swimming or walking

In various settings like at work or on public transport, we can engage in these activities discreetly, the use of headphones, a blessing. Silent singing or imaginative dancing in our minds becomes a delightful way to experience joy moments. We can embrace any of these activities, even when we don't feel like it. In fact, especially when we don't feel like it. That is how we turn our negative jam into a joyful jam.

> In your journal reflect on what you either already practise to stay joyful, or some of the above suggestions you might consider trying.

As we enter God's rest we cease from our own works.

Hebrews 4:10

FINDING REST IN A BUSY WORLD

Chapter 5

FINDING REST IN A BUSY WORLD

How do we define rest? The Oxford Dictionary describes rest as;

a verb

1. Cease work or movement in order to relax. Sleep or recover strength.
2. Be placed or supported so as to stay in a specified position.

a noun

1. An instance or period of resting.
2. An interval of silence of a specified duration. (music)

The intention of this chapter is to focus on the verb; **ceasing to work in order to relax.** We live in a busy world where so much is instant. Instant information, fast food, technological equipment, apps and websites that help us do everything quickly. While many of these technological advances are designed to save us time, it seems the time we save, we tend to fill up with even more tasks. Depending on how we are wired, rest can come very easily to some and not so easily to others. It seems like an oxymoron, but seriously, for some of us, rest is an area that we have to work hard to achieve. If we don't actively work to create time in our schedules to rest, it does not happen.

Being task orientated or an active relaxer, you may relate to writing a list for the day of what you hope to achieve, ticking off as you go? Anything extra you do, you add to your list and tick off? Seriously, that is what I do. Where this comes from, honestly, I don't know. Possibly as a result of being a solo mum for 14 years, raising three young children, while studying to be a teacher and subsequently working as a teacher. Life was so busy! The girls played sport competitively and were often selected for representative teams as well as their usual school teams. Trying to get each child to their respective venues, overseeing their schooling and coping with a very sick child in his early years, all contributed to being a list maker. Study started at 4.00am which was the only time of the day where I could have quiet, uninterrupted time to read and write assignments. This allowed me to be present later in the morning to organise the children for school and after school when we all got home. Add to that being actively involved in our local church and school - my faith community. Thank God for them as they helped and enriched our lives. Many of you will be seeing yourselves in these scenarios.

Do we need to rest and if so, why? When the creator of the universe commands us to rest one day a week, it clearly must be important. *Genesis 2:2-3. On the seventh day God finished His work that He had done.* If God rested, we sure can. I learned this in the first person. In the midst of this very busy season in my life, during my precious quiet time in the morning Bible reading and in prayer, I heard the Lord say, "Rest. Sunday is a day of rest. I have commanded it and I mean it." This didn't feel like a rebuke, but a firm reminder of the commandment to rest one day a week. He knows how busy we can become. He also knows how important rest is to allow the body and mind to recover and rejuvenate. We don't have to be religious about it, but he does command us to set aside time to rest from our busyness in whatever way that is possible.

I hear you saying, "That is all very well for you but I work full time, I have a young family with lots of commitments over the weekend. There are household chores and demands on my time. When do I ever get time to rest?" Truly, I hear you, it sounds like my own heart's cry from some time ago. Like me, possibly you are trying to do too much, or maybe have a very high expectation of how things are done? Consider whether you personally have taken on too much, instead of including all the family to share the tasks around the home. By sharing the load, everyone gets some time to relax. Young couples today are much better at this than my generation, I have observed. Many men are wonderful at sharing the cooking, cleaning and children's needs, which is terrific and the way it should be. Couples today work it out together as they do value social interaction, rest and enjoyable family time. They make it work. Probably because they have watched their mothers slaving away and don't want to go there!

Below are some practical ideas about how to factor rest into your week, however the best place to start is with Him. Whether your quiet time with Him is first thing in the morning or last thing at night, or somewhere in between, take that special time to sit with Him and to spend time reading His Word. With a very young family these moments can be very difficult to create. Kris Vallaton of Bethel Church and School of Supernatural Ministry, found his place was in the bath at the end of the work day. Whatever, or however you can help each other find that time, it is critical for relationship, healing, rest and relaxation. Through that special time He will help direct your path and show you what rest looks like for you in your current circumstances and season of life.

Asheritah Ciuciu of Proverbs 31 Ministries has developed a great acronym for rest.

A guide toward Jesus when we feel overwhelmed.

- **R: Recite God's goodness.** The next time we find ourselves hustling, let's pause to praise God for who He is and what He's already doing (see Psalm 103:1-2). What can we thank Him for? Let's start there.
- **E: Express your neediness.** Then we get honest with God about our struggles and sins, casting our burdens on Him because He cares for us. (1 Peter 5:7)
- **S: Seek His stillness.** Next, we take time to *"be still, and know"* that He is God (Psalm 46:10a, ESV). We quiet our hearts to listen to His still, small voice. Is there anything *He* wants to say to *us*? Are there any burdens or to-dos He's asking us to lay down?
- **T: Trust His faithfulness.** Finally, we declare our confidence that our good God, who began a good work in us, will be faithful to complete it. (Philippians 1:6)

If you find yourself still seeking guidance on how to incorporate rest into your week, consider these practical suggestions to make rest a feasible practice, even in the midst of our busy lives.

Some tips can be taken from Jewish communities. When they are approaching the Sabbath where they literally don't cook, clean or do anything else, they prepare everything beforehand. Not a bad idea to have a meal prepared the day before that only needs to be heated or served. The important household chores are shared and done before the designated rest day. Plan with the family, have a round table discussion. Brainstorm the ways each of you individually, and as a family, want to enjoy your rest day. What do you all need to do to make sure it happens? Circle the rest days on the calendar and designate each family member's idea, so everyone feels valued that their suggestion is being actioned. It does not have to be something you all do together. It may be a day when everyone gets to do their own rest activity. It could look very different for each individual. That is okay. The outcome is still rest.

It is about being kind to ourselves and recharging the batteries so we don't run the risk of burnout. As someone who did just that, I can tell you it takes a long time to recover. It is much better to prevent it by recognising the importance of rest. The reason for my burnout was not only because of what I was trying to fit into a day, but because the amount of time I was spending in my quiet time with God was dramatically reduced. In effect, I had come out from under the protection and covering that rest time with Him brings. Being hit left, right and centre instead of quiet calm, restful moments in His presence. Time with Him is not only rest, but restoration.

> "Come to me, all you who are weary and burdened, and I will give you rest. Take my yoke upon you and learn from me, for I am gentle and humble in heart, and you will find rest for your souls. For my yoke is easy and my burden is light"
> Matthew 11:28-30, NIV

In your journal take a moment with Jesus and work through REST. What are some ways that you are going to be kind to yourself this week by ways of resting?

God, you're such a safe and powerful place to find refuge! You're a proven help in time of trouble.

Psalms 46:1

STAY IN REST WHILE THE STORM IS RAGING

Chapter 6

STAYING IN REST WHILE THE STORM IS RAGING

In this chapter we will focus on the second definition of rest as a verb - **Be placed or supported so as to stay in a specified position.**

Life will bring its challenges. They could be literal storms that cause damage or loss of life to our property or our loved ones. There can be a financial crisis, job loss, health diagnosis. The list is endless as to what situations may be regarded as a storm. Situations like these are often referred to as a storm because they can rise unexpectedly.

Picture yourself in a small boat on a calm sea, the sun is glinting off the water and warming your whole body. So peaceful, relaxing and enjoyable. You could stay here indefinitely. Suddenly, something shifts. There is a cooling effect to the gentle breeze. In fact it is no longer a gentle breeze but a wind that is getting stronger. Above you the blue sky is transforming into tones of angry purple and grey. A change is certainly in the air. Those little waves you were delighting in are being whipped up into something much more ominous. The noise of the wind is now deafening. A wild storm is on its way and it is approaching far more quickly than you could ever have imagined. What do you decide to do next?

In the above scenario most of us would most likely get rowing, or start up the motor and get to a place of safety as quickly as we can. That is exactly the response we need when we are hit by the storms of life. Where is that safe place? Who is that safe place?

Let us reconsider the definition of rest. **Be placed or supported so as to stay in a specified position.** How can we maintain a state of rest when surrounded by turmoil? Often, when life's storms hit, our default response is to either lash out, complain about our victim status, or seek refuge under the covers. We may vent frustrations, assign blame, and recount our woes to anyone willing to listen, perpetuating negativity through repetitive conversations and knee-jerk reactions. Many of us have experienced this cycle. It is only when we come to realise the futility of these actions that, as a last resort, we turn to prayer. After exhausting our own efforts, we finally seek Him to provide the help we need.

Many opportunities to put this into practice have presented themselves throughout my life! In the early stages of my faith journey, it took me some time to realise that the most effective approach is to, first and foremost, turn to His Word and to Him. Once armed with the relevant scriptures I sit with the Holy Spirit, settling into the quiet of His presence to seek any leading or prompting. I surrender the entire situation to Him. Over time, He has become my first recourse when faced with problems or storms. I have discovered that relying on His strength enables me to calm the storms far more swiftly than I could ever achieve on my own.

Scripture helps us here. We are encouraged to practise being in a place of peace, holding our position, regardless of what is going on around us. Keeping our eyes fixed on Jesus.

> **Casting all your cares (all your anxieties, all your worries, and all your concerns, once and for all) on Him, for He cares about you (with deepest affection, and watches over you very carefully).**
> **1 Peter 5:7**

It is super important to remember that anything we take to Him, we leave with Him. The second we take it back and start worrying about the problem again, we remove the ability for Him to work in it. He can't work on something we have taken back. So once we give it to Him, we then rest, trust and believe what it says in Romans 8:28. *God works all things for good for those who love Him and are called according to His purposes.* The outcome may differ from what we initially anticipated, but you can be assured that His ways are superior to ours and His solutions benefit not only ourselves, but also others affected.

> **Do not be anxious about anything, but in every situation, by prayer and petition, with thanksgiving, present your requests to God.**
> **Philippians 4: 6**

So how do we do that? We go to Jesus, our safe place, we tell him about our storm, our problem, our diagnosis. You may have your own way that you get quiet with Jesus and hear Him speak to you. However, I have found that the <u>4 Keys to Hearing God's Voice</u> by Mark Virkler, of Communion with God Ministries, has been very helpful.

The 4 Keys are:

- Quiet yourself down
- Fix your eyes on Jesus
- Tune into spontaneous flowing thoughts
- Journal, write down what you hear

In your journal, try this activation.

- Quiet yourself down
- Picture yourself in the cave or somewhere where you feel sheltered and safe. Come back to being in the boat when the storm starts. We are trying to get to safety as quickly as we can. Imagine that you pull the boat up on shore and see a cave in the rocks where you can enter and are completely sheltered from the wind and the rain. You are warm, dry and safe. He is in that place. That place out of the wind and rain, away from the storm. A place of safety to come, sit, catch your breath and tell Him what is going on.
- Fix your eyes on Jesus -Imagine Jesus is there with you.
- Tune into spontaneous flowing thoughts - Smile because this will help you tune into His thoughts instead of your own.
- Journal, write down what you hear - Talk to Him, tell Him what is going on and ask Him what you should be doing right now. Then as soon as you start to either see a picture or hear words, write them down.

In this process you will feel His peace, His love and the stillness that is Him. You will feel comforted by His presence and be uplifted by what He says to you or what He shows you. What you write down will be a great source of comfort. This is not something that you only do once. You can do this daily, more than once a day, whenever you need to commune with Him.

It is from this place of rest that you will stay in a position where you will cope so much better with the storm around you. Will this take the storm away? Not always straight away, but it will help you stay at peace, make wise decisions, and be calm and strong throughout. If you start to feel tossed around by the waves again, you can go back and read the words you have written and feel the reassurance that is needed. This is how you can be "placed and supported in a specified position of rest" in the storm.

But the one who always listens to me will live undisturbed in a heavenly peace. Free from fear, confident and courageous, you will rest unafraid and sheltered from the storms of life.

Proverbs 1:33

FINDING PEACE IN THE STORM

Chapter 7
FINDING PEACE IN THE STORM

Rest and peace share a close connection. What is peace? Consider what peace looks like for you. Is it experienced as a physical place, an encounter, an emotion, or perhaps a specific person? Take a moment to reflect and record what peace looks like for you.

As previously identified, rest takes on various forms - it can be physical and also a state of holding everything in a pattern of trust, surrendering it all to Jesus and finding assurance in the understanding that He is in control. It is residing in His care. This place of rest often accompanies a profound sense of peace. From this knowledge, let us look at what peace looks like and why it is crucial to experience it, especially in the midst of life's storms. Accessing this peace is the skill required in navigating challenging times.

In various aspects of life, from catching a plane to taking an Uber or taxi, undergoing surgery, or enjoying rides in a theme park, our trust is inherently placed in another human being. The source of our peace often lies in the confidence we have in these individuals or systems. We trust that the plane will take off and land safely, the surgery will be skillfully conducted by an experienced surgeon, and we will emerge unharmed. We rely on the well-maintained condition of the vehicle we are travelling in and the expertise of those operating the equipment. If we can confidently place our trust in these circumstances, consider the depth of trust we can place in God when we surrender everything into His care.

> **Casting all your cares (all your anxieties, all your worries, and all your concerns, once and for all) on Him, for He cares about you (with deepest affection, and watches over you very carefully).**
> **1 Peter 5**

Peace is that serene place where worry and anxiety find no foothold, irrespective of our circumstances. It is a state of rest where we entrust our cares and concerns to someone or something, steadfast in the belief that goodness will prevail. Peace is also a person. His name is Father God, Jesus, and the Holy Spirit.

Psalm 23, below, paints a picture of finding peace in the storm. It is a place of relationship, trust, comfort and support in the midst of challenges and adversaries. It is knowing you are not alone, facing nothing by yourself.

> **The Lord is my shepherd, I lack nothing. He makes me lie down in green pastures, He leads me beside quiet waters, He refreshes my soul. He guides me along the right paths for his name's sake. Even though I walk through the darkest valley, I will fear no evil, for you are with me; your rod and your staff, they comfort me. You prepare a table before me in the presence of my enemies. You anoint my head with oil; my cup overflows. Surely your**

> goodness and love will follow me all the days of my life, and I will dwell in the house of the Lord forever.
> Psalm 23

This psalm has been a great comfort to me, epitomising the truth and revelation of who He is. Within its tranquil setting, I have visually experienced meeting with Jesus. In my sanctified imagination, I see a scene of waving grass by a brook where we reside on a picnic blanket, either my head in His lap or His head in mine under the shade of a huge tree, whose canopy seems to act as protection. It is a place where I experience great peace. In His presence is peace. He is the one who calms the storms.

> Then He got into the boat and his disciples followed him. Suddenly a furious storm came up on the lake, so that the waves swept over the boat. But Jesus was sleeping. The disciples went and woke him, saying, "Lord, save us! We're going to drown! "He replied, "You of little faith, why are you so afraid?" Then he got up and rebuked the winds and the waves, and it was completely calm. The men were amazed and asked, "What kind of man is this? Even the winds and the waves obey him!"
> Matthew 8:23-27

Having read this scripture numerous times, my main focus has always been on the power of Jesus to literally override the elements and calm the storm. However, recently, the revelation that really resonated with me was that "Jesus was sleeping." There was a storm going on, yet Jesus had his head on a pillow at the back of the boat, sound asleep. There was nothing to fear here. This was a significant discovery for me. Such is the nature of Jesus. This is the picture I visualise when faced with challenges. Walking with Jesus is like that. His response which becomes our response is to rest, be at peace. From this place of peace we will know what to do, if anything. The disciples were panicking - likely the usual response for most of us. They were with Jesus, this person who knows how to calm storms and materialise miracles. Why wasn't he doing anything? There was some teaching the disciples needed to grasp here. They had witnessed so many miracles at the hand of Jesus and even in the case of feeding the five thousand, at their own hands. Everything they saw Him do, Jesus was demonstrating what they too could do. Jesus clearly was expecting them to trust that Jesus was with them and he had previously demonstrated what to do to calm the wind and the waves. They had authority in His name to do so. So do we.

Walking in relationship with Jesus is to co-labour with Him. Knowing He is with us, we have the opportunity to commune with Him whenever we want to about anything and everything. He is the power within us, the peace within us. He abides in us and we abide in Him. He is the source of our peace and He never leaves us nor forsakes us. He is as close as our hand and goes with us wherever we go. This is important to take hold of.

Our mindset can be that we get along doing life and when we need Him, we call. However, as he is in the boat with us and goes where we go, we can be at peace, because He is at peace. We can trust that when we are in relationship with Him, talk to Him, share our life with Him, He will work in our situations, if we ask. We have His Word, full of promises to confirm this.

> **For He will command his angels concerning**
> **you to guard you in all your ways.**
> **Psalm 91:11**

We are under the watchful care of angels to protect, guard and minister to us. When we take everything to Him, seeking comfort in His promises within His Word, we can find rest in His peace, assured that He has everything under control.

Only a matter of weeks ago, three quite dramatic events occurred with loved ones in my family. Each one brought its own shock and emotional response. Firstly, one of our grandsons was very unwell, with suspected Type 1 Diabetes. A rush to the Emergency Department resulted in him being admitted, the diagnosis being confirmed. It is such a shock to see your loved ones become ill and given a life sentence diagnosis. So sad to see my daughter and son-in-law grieve for what their son was going through, but being so strong for him. A couple of days later, our other grandson presented in the same Emergency Department with what seemed like a heart issue. Only a matter of days after that, our son also had a crisis moment. This was a storm and winds were coming from three different directions. However, in the midst of this storm, perfect peace resided throughout. In spite of how things appeared, there was a high level of trust that our prayers would be answered and that God would work all things for good. *Romans 8:28.* Grateful for the privilege to sit with God and surrender everything, we find comfort in His presence, experiencing His abiding peace. It is more than knowledge, it is a tangible encounter. Like a child confiding in a loved and trusted parent, we are invited to reside in that place. Sharing our concerns with Him brings not only comfort but also the assurance that solutions will follow, ushering in a deep sense of peace. From that place of peace, we can be a strong tower to each member of the family, friends and each other. With hearts full of peace, trust and belief, we encourage, uplift and support others through their circumstances, knowing that everything will work out okay.

> In your journal take a moment to reflect on times when you have been battered by a storm but have felt His peace.
>
> If you have struggled to find peace in difficult situations, what might you practise going forward to build your relationship with Jesus?
>
> Consider writing down some of the scriptures mentioned in this chapter. As you reflect on them as a source of peace and strength, may they equip you for any storm that might present itself in the future.

You will keep in perfect peace those whose minds are steadfast, because they trust in you.

Isaiah 26:3 (NIV)

WARRING THROUGH REST

Chapter 8
WARRING THROUGH REST

Having explored definitions of rest, let us consider 'warring'. Warring means a state of conflict between two or more people or groups.

At times, it seems as though we are engaged in a mental battlefield, combating anxiety, worry and troubling thoughts that revolve around how to deal with issues. Often this leads to an emotional roller coaster ride. How do we manage the thoughts bombarding us and maintain our sense of rest?

> For the weapons of our warfare are not fleshly
> but powerful through God for the tearing down of
> strongholds. We are tearing down false arguments.
> 2 Cor. 10:4-5

What weapons are available to us, metaphorically, to counter this internal onslaught? The weapons mentioned are not physical swords or shields but spiritual tools like prayer, faith and the Word of God. The emphasis is on relying on God's strength and guidance to overcome spiritual challenges and opposition.

When our son, aged five, was diagnosed with a brain tumour, we were immediately asked to present ourselves at the Children's hospital for tests and preparation for surgery. I can still recall the numb, heavy feeling in my legs as we entered the ward, hardly daring to look around and take in the enormity of the situation, not really wanting to go there, but knowing we had to. After admission and all the usual testing that takes place, we met with the Neurosurgeon. A nurse was present as he described the type of tumour we were dealing with, the nature of the surgery, and how it would be carried out, followed by the potential risks that can take place with this type of surgery. There were seven different ways that he could be permanently affected post-surgery, including ways that he could pass away. Certainly a perfect opportunity for a battle of the mind to begin!

The Neurosurgeon asked if there were any questions. There being none, he left. Within a minute or so, the nurse, having studied me closely, started to repeat the seven potential outcomes that could occur. When I realised what she was doing, I stopped her at the end of number two and said, "I heard very clearly everything the surgeon said and have taken it on board. However, these risks will be given no further thought unless we actually have to deal with each or all of them. We will cross that bridge only if we have to." Because my response was probably hard to read during and after the clinical laying out of potential risk, I think she assumed that I had not understood what the enormous consequences could be. This was understandable from her perspective as she would have been trained to ensure that patients know what the possibilities are.

A relatively new believer at the time, I was putting my trust in God that He would get us through. There would be no battlefield of the mind. I was not prepared to agonise over 'what ifs'. There was enough going on, and one five year old boy needed his mum to be courageous and help him get through what he needed to. My belief was that whatever we needed to face going forward, we would be given the strength we needed for each new day, so grateful to be able to lay all of that in God's hands and just deal with what was required at the time. There would be no worrying or anxiety. Remarkably, only one of those outcomes occurred and even then, it was to a very minor degree. Praise God. I could have used up so much emotional energy, getting myself wound up about all the possible risks that did not happen.

The most powerful weapon at our disposal is the Word of God. Turning His Word into a decree and proclaiming it over our circumstances is powerful. *So shall My Word be that goes forth from My mouth; It shall not return to Me void, But it shall accomplish what I please, and it shall prosper in the thing for which I sent it. Isaiah 55:11* NKJV. In other words when God speaks, His Word carries authority, truth and creative power. It is a declaration that what follows is not just human words but a divine proclamation. 'It shall not return to me void' assures us that God's Word will not come back empty or without results. Powerful!

The wonderful thing about our modern technology and the easy access to information through the internet, is that we can search up scripture which applies to our situation.

> **And this same God who takes care of me will supply all your needs from His glorious riches, which have been given to us in Christ Jesus.**
> **Philippians 4:19**

> **The blessing of the Lord makes a person rich, and He adds no sorrow with it.**
> **Proverbs 10:22**

> **And God will generously provide all you need.**
> **2 Corinthians 9:8**

Just like that, you have a weapon of warfare at your disposal to use as a decree to declare aloud over your circumstances. Often we can feel powerless to do anything. However, having His Word to use as a 'weapon' over our situation shifts the place of power. We stand in faith that He will work in our situation to see a solution. We can stand strong, robed in our full armour of God as described in Paul's letter to the Ephesians, knowing His Word is working on our behalf.

> **Therefore put on the full armour of God, so that when the day of evil comes, you may be able to stand your ground, and after you have done everything, to stand. Stand firm then, with the belt of truth buckled around your waist, with the breastplate of righteousness in place, and with your feet fitted with the readiness that comes from the gospel of peace. In addition to all this, take up the shield of faith, with which you can extinguish all the flaming arrows of the evil one. Take the helmet of salvation and the sword of the Spirit, which is the Word of God.**
> **Ephesians 6:13-17**

Having done all this – stand. This is where we now war in rest. So having done our decrees over our situation and over the battlefield in our mind, we rest. Our armour is resting, knowing that the Word is working it out. We are protected by rest, knowing that we have used our best weapon for peace in our situation. The adversary seeks to mess up our minds, to have us so troubled and anxious that we move from faith to fear. His strategy is to divert our focus from Jesus to our circumstances, causing us to feel as though we are sinking instead of walking on the water. However, when we intentionally stay in peace and rest in the midst of life's storms, we thwart the enemy's attempt to impact us. It is resting in God's promises, casting cares or troubles on Him, believing in the Word to manifest in our situation, that becomes our most effective weapon. Our warfare is waged from a posture of rest.

> Reflecting on your life, have you encountered or are you currently facing a battle that requires breakthrough? Return to your journal, take a moment to list the strategies you have used to cope with the situation. Evaluate how effective these strategies have been and how they differ or compare to some of the strategies mentioned in this chapter. Consider looking up some scriptures that can be declared over your current battlefield. Start declaring them over your situation today and then rest in peace, knowing that you have released the power of His Word.

Listen to my testimony: I cried to God in my distress,
and he answered me. He freed me from all my fears!

Psalm 34:4

BEING AN OVERCOMER: FROM FEAR TO FAITH

Chapter 9

BEING AN OVERCOMER: FROM FEAR TO FAITH

What does it mean to be an overcomer? A person who overcomes something: one who succeeds in dealing with or gaining control of some problem or difficulty.

In the previous chapter we looked at effective strategies to take us from feeling powerless in our situation, to applying God's Word which empowers us in our circumstances. A great place to start in response to the question "How do we move from being a victim to becoming an overcomer?" A victim is someone who is tricked or duped by a scam or hoax; a person who *has come to feel helpless and passive in the face of misfortune or ill-treatment. (Oxford Dictionary)*

Many of us have felt like a victim at one time or another. A set of circumstances, seemingly, beyond our control, can make us feel fearful about our future. It can be a reason to go down a rabbit hole of self-criticism, blame, or asking the wrong questions that keep us bound in victim mode.

The first step to taking back control and power is to ask, "What do I need at this time to move through, above and beyond this?" Our first place is always Jesus. He is the answer to every question and the solution to every problem. So often we run around doing all sorts of things or we do nothing at all. It has been my experience, if we had just sat with Jesus, sought his leading and guiding for a solution, we would have been a great deal better off. Often in the seeking and praying, creative solutions and practical ideas come to mind which direct our next steps. Faith is the opposite of fear, so how do we turn from fear to faith? We talked earlier about who we put our trust in. When we understand our identity as sons and daughters of God, positioning ourselves in faith becomes a natural response. Knowing that we belong to a loving Father, who is inherently good and kind, allows us to trust that He always has our best interests at heart.

> **For I know the plans I have for you. They are
> to prosper you for a hope and future.
> Jeremiah 29:11**

> **God works all things for good for those who love
> Him and are called according to His purposes.
> Romans 8:28**

> **I can do all things through Christ who strengthens me.
> Philippians 4:13**

My husband had been retired for a year from secondary school teaching, when he was approached by the Head of Department of Technology at our local secondary school. Would my husband be interested in being a part time teacher for six months, with a view to that being extended to twelve months? They were short staffed. He made the decision to take up the offer. He seemed to really enjoy the classes, the close proximity of the school to home and the connection with teaching colleagues again. However, because of a funding shortfall due to lower than expected student numbers by mid-year, he was to finish after six months and not proceed for the rest of the year. He was under the impression that even though his part time classes had finished, it was more than likely he would be required to do relieving work in the second half of the year. However, when the new term started, a few weeks had passed and there were no requests forthcoming. He was starting to think he had done something wrong. Maybe there had been some sort of misunderstanding? Then I noticed little lists around the home of things my husband could make in his workshop to sell. He also seemed to be a bit agitated.

An opportunity presented itself where I was able to mention what I was noticing and to ask if everything was alright? On the surface he wasn't aware that he was behaving differently. The discussion brought to light that subconsciously, my husband had been missing the income, concerned about our future and feeling a responsibility to bring more income into the household. As I am still working part-time and we receive a pension, I reassured him that he need not be concerned about money. We don't have much, but we have all we need. This was an important reminder for us to recognise that fear was the opposite of faith. It highlighted the importance of placing our trust in God, our provider, who consistently comes up with creative ideas and ways to generate income. He knows our needs. We were able to recall the countless instances where He had faithfully come through for us in the past, many of which are detailed in my previous book "Is that You Papa? Tuning into the Voice of God.". Assured again that His provision has been consistent throughout the years, we offered heartfelt thanks in prayer. We were so grateful for the numerous times He had come through in our finances over the years, fostering a sense of peace within us both as we reflected on the abundance of His blessings we have experienced.

Later that week, my husband said "You need to sit down. A couple of miracles have happened." When he opened his emails there was one from the school asking him if he was available for relieving the following week. Then he was checking our bank account for something and found that he had been paid a substantial teacher's back pay. That was our Papa God demonstrating how He provides. If my husband had any residue of fear, he certainly didn't after that. Our faith in His provision proved very trustworthy as He yet again, provided.

Reaffirming that when we stand in the knowledge of being a son or daughter of God we can stand strong and be courageous in adversity, because we know He has our back.

> **Have I not commanded you? Be strong and courageous.**
> **Do not be afraid; do not be discouraged for the**
> **Lord your God will be with you wherever you go.**
> **Joshua 1:9**

Armed with the knowledge of who we are in God, we can now review the question " What do I need at this time to move through, above and beyond this?" Our first step was with Jesus, moving us from fear to faith. Now, what are practical steps we need to take? These may have come when you sat with Jesus. They may come afterwards, but taking back the power involves looking at all we can do practically to move forward. This might come in the form of a conversation that needs to occur, such as my husband and I had. Depending on the issue, it could be making some enquiries with organisations or agencies that specialise in the situation you may be facing, who could advise you as to what you need to be doing.

Many years ago, we read a book called <u>The Barefoot Investor</u> by Scott Pape. It is an excellent practical guide into getting out of debt, buying your first home and investing for your retirement. In the first chapter he talks about how people can often have more than one credit card and each one is maxed out, putting people under a great deal of financial pressure. He shows a very practical way of taking the first step to reducing that debt and the goals going forward. He says that what he is showing people will not take them out of debt straight away, but will empower them by having a plan to get out of debt and therefore, taking back control. In essence that is what we are doing here. You may not be able to change the circumstances you have found yourself in immediately, but by standing in your position as a daughter or son of God, knowing He wants the very best for you, seeking Jesus and taking steps to seek help with practical solutions to move forward, the power is back in your own hands. You are no longer a victim. You are an overcomer.

> In your journal reflect on times in your life where you have felt powerless to change something. Were you able to turn from fear to faith in your situation? Was there anything practical that could be done? Write some examples of what worked for you.
>
> If the feeling of powerlessness has remained in your situation or you are currently in a place of feeling powerless, write down the scriptures above and meditate on them. What are a few practical steps that you might consider taking that would make you feel like you have taken the power back?

> Whatever was written beforehand is meant to instruct us in how to live. The Scriptures impart to us encouragement and inspiration so that we can live in hope and endure all things.
>
> Romans 15:4

KEEPING HEARTS OF HOPE IN DIFFICULT TIMES

Chapter 10

KEEPING HEARTS OF HOPE IN DIFFICULT TIMES

What is hope? Hope is a feeling of expectation and desire for a particular thing to happen. It is grounds for believing that something good may happen.

> For in this hope, we were saved. But hope that is seen is no hope at all. Who hopes for what they already have? But if we hope for what we do not yet have, we wait for it patiently.
> Romans 8:24-25

The opposite of hope is hopelessness, which is having no expectation of good or success, incapable of redemption or improvement or not susceptible to remedy or cure. It is where we cannot see beyond our current circumstances. How does hope compare to faith?

> **Faith is the confidence that what we hope for will actually happen; it gives us assurance about things we cannot see.**
> **Hebrews 11:1 NIV**

To summarise, while faith involves belief and trust, often with a focus on the present, hope is about positive anticipation for the future. Both concepts are essential in providing a sense of purpose, optimism, and resilience in various aspects of life. Hope is always looking towards good outcomes. Hope wrapped in faith is an assurance, a confidence of what we hope for will come to pass. Hope reduces feelings of helplessness, it takes us out of our situation and helps us look beyond it. With hope we gather strength for the now, hoping this is just a season and will pass. Faith takes that hope and builds trust for this time to pass and for something better to come.

> **Hope deferred makes the heart sick, but**
> **a longing fulfilled is a tree of life.**
> **Proverbs 13:12**

Have you been waiting a long time for something to come to pass? How do we position ourselves while waiting? For our miracle, our breakthrough, there are little things we can do along the way which help keep our hearts full of hope. Little steps like being thankful for each tiny thing. Little successes, no matter how small. Like refraining from putting dates or timeframes around the hoped-for end. This will avoid disappointment or discouragement if the date comes and goes and the breakthrough has not yet arrived.

In Chris Gore's book <u>The Perfect Gift; Seeing the child, not the condition</u> he says:

> "Learn how to celebrate every breakthrough and stay in the place of being in the awe of God. As parents and caregivers of children with special needs, we can have a lot of negative situations

come at us and it can become very easy to go to a place of discouragement and hopelessness. However, when we can keep our eyes on what has happened and what is happening, versus focusing on what hasn't happened yet, we can find ourselves living in a place of encouragement."

He goes on to say, "With our daughter, we get excited when she makes a new sound, sleeps well, or feeds herself a potato chip. All these moments are significant to us." Chris Gore was the Director of Healing Ministries at Bethel Church, California for 20 odd years before taking up God's call to return to New Zealand to usher in a healing revival in our nation. Thank you, Chris.

It was truly heartwarming to witness such a lovely illustration of what Chris mentioned, in our own family. Recently, when our eldest grandson was diagnosed with Type 1 Diabetes, I was deeply moved as our daughter shared her gratitude amidst the initial shock. When the school phoned expressing concern about his health, she felt thankful for following her gut instincts and heading straight to the Medical Centre. Gratitude extended to the ambulance guy who having triaged him before, swiftly recognised the severity of the situation and communicated the urgency to the Emergency Department. Appreciation continued for the hospital staff's quick response, admitting him directly into Paediatrics instead of the High Dependency unit due to his age. This decision placed him under the Paediatrician on duty, for whom they were so grateful. In the midst of uncertainty, she expressed how grateful she was for the loving support of family.

Later she continued sharing how grateful she and her husband were for every little step. Every little success that their son was having, dealing with his new diagnosis. Every professional who has now become part of the team to help them navigate his condition going forward. Does this mean that they were not reeling from shock, were not heartbroken at the sudden onslaught of testing, injecting and dietary considerations required for their son going forward? No, they were experiencing all these emotions. However, they were able to take strength from celebrating the little things. Being grateful for what they had, not for what had been taken away or was not happening.

Another helpful way of keeping a heart of hope in difficult times is not only celebrating all the little things and being grateful, but also keeping our eyes on the now and the future rather than being tempted to look back and wallow in the pain of the diagnosis, or the change in circumstances. It can be very easy to look back at what once was and start to feel discouraged, angry, hurt, or even bitter and resentful. The only reason we should look back is to see how far we have come. All those little things we have celebrated, we can look back and say, wow, they might be little things, but that is progress.

> **But those who hope in the Lord will renew their strength.
> They will soar on wings like eagles; they will run and
> not grow weary; they will walk and not be faint.
> Isaiah 40:31**

In your journal, write down all the things that right now, you are grateful for. Reflect on what you have written then celebrate.

I have loved you with an everlasting love; I have drawn you with unfailing kindness.

Jeremiah 3:13 (NIV)

THE POWER OF HIS LOVE; LEARNING TO OVERCOME THROUGH LOVE

Chapter 11

THE POWER OF HIS LOVE; LEARNING TO OVERCOME THROUGH LOVE

The power and importance of love cannot be overstated. Belonging is the most basic need of every human being but is followed very closely by love. How many are living life without knowing what it truly means to be loved, unconditionally? To feel seen, because they are loved. How many have not only known they are loved by the actions of loved ones around them, but have been told they are loved?

When I started ministering to people who needed healing, it came as such a surprise to see so many people with physical ailments, who feel unseen or unlovable. My reality, as the youngest of four children, was growing up knowing how loved I was. Our Dad adored us and was a hugger, we were greeted and farewelled with a hug and celebrated with a hug. He was quick to express his pride in our achievements and for just being who we are. Mum was not a hugger but she was a very positive person, who saw the glass half full as opposed to being half empty. She was always very encouraging about our plans and ideas, there was no doubt in my mind that I was loved.

Therefore, when I came to faith, when I was born again, it was not a difficult step for me to believe in a loving father. His love has the power to forgive, heal, set people free, transform families and communities and restore relationships. So many people struggle to see God as a loving Father because they have not experienced what it is like to have love expressed openly, or even to receive love of any kind. Not surprisingly, their image of Him can be one of a disciplinarian that is always looking to trip us up, condemn and punish us.

One of my greatest delights is to hear the heart of the Father for others. In the School of Faith, there are numerous opportunities to discern God's voice for others; it is deeply ingrained in our culture. During a particular season I found myself in gatherings, regularly prompted to convey a simple yet profound message: 'I see you. I love you.' A true reflection of what the Father is expressing to each one of us. To be seen and not feel invisible, is like being enveloped in an embrace, held secure in that knowledge. In many instances, He guides us to share His thoughts with others from His heart. Witnessing individuals break down in tears as they hear, perhaps for the first time, how deeply loved they are and how proud their Heavenly Father is of them is such a blessing. Observing their reactions as we call out the gold within them is transformative. The realisation that they are truly seen, valued and loved is evidenced in the countenance on their faces.

> **How priceless is your unfailing love, O God: People take refuge in the shadow of your wings.**
> **Psalms 36:7**

An important part of our life's journey is to posture our hearts to remain in love. At times this can be challenging, but it is possible with His help and with the help of loving friends and family. When I have been in very painful circumstances, He speaks to my heart through songs. One of those defining moments occurred not long after the heartbreaking diagnosis for my son mentioned previously. This happened in the early stages of my Christian journey, surrounded by the warmth and support of a loving faith community. We were nearing the end of the Sunday morning service, the introductory notes to 'The Power of Your Love' by Hillsong Worship began to play. Tentatively, I started to sing the first verse, but as I embraced the chorus, a powerful wave of faith and emotion swept over me.

Sobbing through the rest of the song, something happened in my heart. It was like the whole congregation was helping me as they sang so strongly those powerful words. My heart was receiving every word as a healing balm for the brokenness of a mother grieving for her young son. While remaining positive and filled with hope, it was also a time of working through grief from shocking news. In that moment my strength returned, my spirit was uplifted and upheld. This was not a journey I was facing alone.

In another instance of deep sadness when a newfound relationship had ended abruptly, I found myself driving through tears to a favourite place by the Petone foreshore. Pulling into the carpark, a weather-beaten, wooden bench was drawing me to reside upon it. Normally, the picture perfect scenery of a tranquil harbour sparkling in the sunlight, grey sand, squawking seagulls, laughter and splashing heard from paddling children, dogs trotting along with exercising owners, the salty smell on the breeze and feeling the embrace of the enveloping bush clad hills would have been my focus and a delight to behold. However, so deep was the pain in that moment, the only place my focus was on, was my feet upon the sandy ground beneath them. While in that seemingly defeated pose, a melody began to weave its way into my consciousness, the first lines of Shout to the Lord.

As each line of the song was playing through my mind and heart, my head slowly started to lift. I became aware of not only the words of the song and the melody, but the beautiful scenery all around me was ministering to my very sore heart. He was lifting my head, showing me all the beauty that was around me. The song ministered to my heart and mind and reminded me that this was not being faced alone, that He loves me, that my focus is on Him and He is my healer, my comforter, my all.

Having sung that song about three times, I was ready to stand up and head home, feeling mostly healed, whole, uplifted and strengthened. Ready to face the world again. He truly is our comfort, our shelter, tower of refuge and strength. That is the power of His love.

It may help to know that this song came from loss too. Darlene Zschech of Hillsong wrote this song from her pain of miscarrying her baby. Through her grief God gave her the lyrics and melody for this song which mended her heart too. Our God knows what pain and grief looks like and what we need to walk through and overcome it.

> **This is how God showed His love among us: He sent His one and only Son into the world that we might live through Him. This is love: not that we loved God, but that He loved us and sent His Son as an atoning sacrifice for our sins.**
> 1 John 4:9-10

In your journal reflect on how you know you are loved. If you are struggling to find any language or thoughts to describe what feeling loved looks like, consider looking up the songs I have mentioned and playing them through while you ask Jesus to come into your heart and help you know how loved you are. Write down what takes place during this time.

But instead, be kind and affectionate toward one another. Has God graciously forgiven you? Then graciously forgive one another in the depths of Christ's love.

Ephesians 4:32

FORGIVING THE UNFORGIVABLE

Chapter 12

FORGIVING THE UNFORGIVABLE

Are there any actions or behaviours that you would consider impossible to forgive? Any circumstance whereby you might be able to forgive but unlikely to forget?

In 2021 my debut book 'Is that You Papa? Tuning into the Voice of God' was published. It was never in my life plan to write a book and certainly not one that contained aspects of my life story. However, God had another plan and so a new season was born, where waking at 3.00am most mornings became my new normality, with text running through my mind that needed to be recorded. This was not to be ignored, so I went with it. As it unfolded, it was apparent that it was shaping up as a memoir with a message. I realised that all the stories were demonstrating the different ways that God speaks, the wonderful ways He has spoken to me over the years and the outcome of hearing His voice. Having come to the point where it seemed to be complete, I still had no clue as to the purpose for writing. Was this a cathartic exercise, or was it something more? Maybe it was for my children? Something to be put away in a folder in my desk for them to read after I am gone? Being a very personal story because He is a very relational God, I was not sure anyone else would want to read it.

Surprisingly, at the point of completion He mentioned the names of some people whom I admire and respect and told me to get them to write a foreword for my book. Perplexed, my thoughts went to 'Why do I need a foreword for a book that only my children will read?' Ignoring my question, the name of one of our Book Club members popped into my mind, with the suggestion she be given the draft to read through and give some feedback. Now my interest was really piqued as I realised there was another purpose for this book that was wider than the audience of three.

The book was published. It was an exciting but very vulnerable experience to have stories from your life available for anyone interested to read. Out of the blue I got a phone call from a man who said he was calling from Delaware in America. He named the company he was working for and said my book had been brought to his attention. Immediately my thoughts darted straight to suspicion. "So how come, among the thousands of books published and released monthly, does my little book get brought to your attention? It is more likely that someone is searching for debut authors, especially faith based books to entice them into a scam." He hastily reassured me that his call was sincere, they were a legitimate company who assisted authors to get their new books out there. They had marketing strategies that were tried and tested. The promise of a marketing video promoting my book, sent to my inbox within 24 hours would be evidence of their skill and expertise. As I still continued to challenge him and his services, he offered further reassurance by telling me to check them out on the internet and on YouTube to see other work they had produced. Even if my decision was not to go with them, the video would be free for me to use. Of course I checked out the website, some of the video clips as suggested. Everything seemed authentic. However, as the company that published my book was already working on a marketing package for me, I declined his services explaining that the existing marketing package in place needed to be given its own opportunity to run. He asked if he could check in again in January to see how the marketing was going?

True to his word he made contact in January enquiring how the marketing was going? By this time it was evident that the marketing package my publisher had put together was unimpressive, lack-lustre and very disappointing. The only sales were the ones I was generating from my own stock. Some creative marketing assistance was necessary to sell the stock my publisher had pressured me to purchase. For this reason, after fresh discussion with the man from Delaware, we accepted the proposal of their producing a video and our paying for an email marketing package. Then followed, after some weeks, a proposal for my book to be published in China. I was incredulous at this suggestion. How on earth would you publish a Christian book in a communist country to sell there. Even with the very professional example of the book cover written in Chinese and so called emails from the publisher in China, I just wasn't convinced. Red flags were flying again. His totally calm, professional demeanour remained throughout. His constant reassurance on the importance of checking out the legitimacy of the company in China, reading articles about people who had published Christian books in China must be carried out in order for us to make a decision. The offer seemed feasible, the distribution and price per book to the author was encouraging. A small amount but with strong commitments from bookshops to purchase a small number, meant it would be a steady income.

To cut a very long story short, a story of investigations, seeking advice from other wise folk doing research online, and many telephone conversations with this man from Delaware for more than seven months, we were scammed! My initial gut response was the correct one. It hit very hard! Especially when you feel you have built a rapport with someone. Determined to get to know this man and find out if he truly was genuine, we had many conversations where I asked him about his life and his family. He seemed so sincere. There was even a miraculous moment when a few days before we paid for the proposal, while in conversation he could not go 30 seconds without coughing and was exhausted with it. I prayed for his Covid cough to go. With the prayerful command his cough left immediately. He was healed in Jesus' name. His response was ecstatic. Following on from that, while enjoying the awe and wonder of what just took place, I saw a vision as I was praying with him. A picture of a swordsman, one dressed for a fencing competition. The sword was pointed directly at this man's heart, and I heard "On guard!" I shared this with him.

The morning after we paid the money, on checking our emails and seeing no acknowledgement of the receipt of funds, the realisation was immediate. In my email to him I told him he was better than this and to provide the services instead of stealing the money. My suggestion was that he build a business instead of being a thief, do a good job and let us recommend him so he could grow a legitimate business and be a professional marketer.

There will be many who read this for whom this is also your story, or a story very similar. From this very unpleasant experience, clearly there is much advice I could offer for debut authors, from what I have learned. However, this is not the purpose of this story. This is about forgiveness. How do you forgive someone who scammed you of a decent chunk of your retirement savings after you had built up, what you thought, was a positive business relationship?

When the truth hit, it was such a kick in the guts, the wind was taken out of our sails, feeling so foolish. Curled up in bed, recovering from my own bout of Covid, I instinctively heard the Lord's whisper urging me to "Bless him." Immediately it became clear in my heart that extending blessings to this person who had deceived us was the only fitting response. Believe me, he was blessed many times a day!!! About 30 or so initially. Whenever thoughts of him crossed my mind I uttered, "Bless him Lord. Bless his going out and coming in. Bless his relationships, and his community." Whatever I could think of, I blessed him. It was important to embrace God's ways knowing they are vastly different to the mindset of the world which seeks to get even. Of course in the midst of the blessings, it was important to follow through on the practical steps of reporting the scam with law enforcement authorities in the United States of America who were so helpful. However, the apparent professionalism of the scammers, with seemingly genuine addresses and phone numbers in Delaware, investigations revealed that the company was never in the USA. It seems it was more likely a company in the Philippines operating under false identities and addresses, making them virtually impossible to track down.

> Bearing with one another and, if one has a complaint against another, forgiving each other; as the Lord has forgiven you, so you also must forgive.
> Col 3:13

Reflecting on this scripture, why do you think we need to forgive? Can't we just stay angry? The choice is ours entirely of course. No one can force us to forgive anyone. However, to give a visual picture of what unforgiveness can look like, imagine you have a weighty, timber raft tied around your waist by a large rope cutting into your very being. On that raft is every person that has hurt or caused you offence. Everywhere you go, you are dragging all these people, these personal stories and conversations around with you. The sad thing is, that the person who inflicted the pain is getting on with life, unaffected by our unforgiveness. However, we are still dragging that load around with us.

Matthew and Dennis Linn, S.J wrote a wonderful book called <u>Healing of Memories</u>. They also run special healing retreats and workshops. Here is an excerpt from the Introduction of the book: "Wherever we go, we find people complaining about some behaviour they would like to change but can't: overeating or drinking, smoking or drugs, sexual compulsions, resentments, feelings of rejection and a negative self-image, depression or moods, ingrained fears that choke risk-taking, or habitual patterns of sin. As parents they repeat their own parents' mistakes and thus hurt their children in the same ways that their parents hurt them. Those who beat their children often grew up a battered child themselves. Why? There are many reasons why we do what we don't want to do, but the most common reason for hurting ourselves or another is that someone has hurt us."

It is one thing to say we would like to forgive. It is another entirely to know what that looks like. Firstly, we need to know that deciding to forgive someone is a head decision. It is not something that we wait until we feel like it, as that time may never come. For some people it can just be a matter of deciding to forgive saying, "I forgive you." Then every time the person or event enters the mind, to repeat it. Eventually, the effects of this decision are evident when we come to the realisation that we are no longer in pain and the person no longer has any power over us. For some of us it is not that simple. The Linn brothers share that it is important for some people not to try and forgive too soon. To take some time between the cause and the time to forgive. For some, forgiveness may be a period using various tools to aid the steps towards forgiveness. Below is outlined a possible tool that may help.

Earlier I mentioned Mark Virkler and his very successful <u>4 Keys to Hearing God's Voice</u>. Just recently, while in one of his online workshops he used this process to walk people through inner healing, forgiveness of offence and deep hurt. It was such a moving experience to see participants process and then share back what was revealed and how healing had already started to take place.

In this live class, some shared that the picture they saw was of a childhood memory that was painful. When they asked Jesus where he was in the picture, they saw that He had been right there with them. They weren't alone and with this realisation they either received the inner healing, or with Him, forgave whoever needed forgiving.

Here are the four keys. However, should you enjoy this process, my recommendation is that you visit CWG Ministries online. They have so many free resources on Hearing God's voice and on healing. Their deeper study resources are worth the outlay too.

The four keys:

- Quieten yourself down
- Visualise, picture Jesus
- Tune into flowing, spontaneous thoughts
- Journal or write what you see and hear.

If you are struggling to let something or many things go, I encourage you to give this a try. It is very healing. Even if you don't think you have anything that needs inner healing or any unforgiveness you are holding onto, give it a go anyway.

> Dearest Jesus,
> I pray that the one working through this activation is covered by the Holy Spirit, that peace and grace are so present for a Jesus encounter of the healing kind. In Jesus name. Amen

Activation for Healing of Unforgiveness Using the Four Keys

How to use the four keys in the context of this activation

- Quieten yourself down
- Visualise Jesus
  Ask Him to take you to any time in your life that needs inner healing or forgiveness. Take your time. Now ask Jesus where He is in the picture. If you can't see Jesus, just go with your best guess as to where you sense He is standing or sitting.
- Tune into flowing, spontaneous thoughts of what He might be saying to you. Sit and wait for what He says or shows you.

- Journal or write what you see and hear

Only after you have written everything you have seen and heard, ask Him questions for clarification or understanding. Write down what He answers or presents as a picture for you, or what you sensed was going on. Hopefully this activation will assist with the healing of old wounds, that restoration and transformation to walk in forgiveness is the outcome.

> If you haven't already, take a moment, with your journal in hand and work through the four keys specifically for inner healing and see what Jesus reveals to you. Ask Him questions in the moment, if you need to. Write down what you see and hear.

Confess and acknowledge how you have offended one another and then pray for one another to be instantly healed, for tremendous power is released through the passionate, heartfelt prayer of a godly believer.

James 5:16

LIVING FREE

Chapter 13
LIVING FREE

We have navigated various dimensions of choosing life-giving words, cultivating kindness, renewing our minds, refreshing the way we speak, finding peace and calm in the storms of life and embracing forgiveness. A transformative journey towards living on the bright side of life. The last crucial aspect in breaking free from negativity, is adopting a blame-free lifestyle.

In today's society there is a tendency to seek out someone to blame, often fuelled by the media's approach to news as previously discussed. The internet and social media provide a virtual shield where people feel so much braver to express themselves than they would in person. The culture of blaming others is perpetuated by a mindset whereby pointing the finger elsewhere can often be the norm. It is tempting, even for us, to succumb to this habit, enabling us to feel better about ourselves or our circumstances. However, when we point the finger at someone else, there are three fingers pointing back at us.

> And why worry about a speck in your friend's eye when you have a log in your own eye? How can you think of saying to your friend, 'Let me help you get rid of that speck in your eye,' when you can't see past the log in your own eye? Hypocrite! First get rid of the log in your own eye; then you will see well enough to deal with the speck in your friend's eye.
> Matthew 7:3-5

In April last year our beloved eldest brother, living in Sydney, passed away at 72 years of age, after a battle with cancer. A much-loved father of three and grandfather of three grandsons. A man who loved his family with so much passion and heart, who was so interested in everything we were doing. His fit and healthy lifestyle made it all the more unexpected that he, of all people, would be the one confronted with illness.

Numerous aspects of his decline present opportunities for laying blame, beginning with the unfortunate accident that occurred in early lockdown. Knocked off his motor scooter, bounced over the bonnet of a car taking a wrong turn, landing on the road resulting in shattering sections of his femur. His solitary journey through surgery, recovery and subsequent rehabilitation unfolded during stringent Covid restrictions. The burden of staying strong, and maintaining a positive mental attitude in the face of adversity was compounded by the absence of loved ones, denied company and support that could have uplifted his spirit during a tough time, shared by many others grappling with injuries or illnesses in that period. Enduring a long rehabilitation, he fought to reclaim his fitness and rebuild his life, a feat he accomplished admirably. However, just when he appeared fit and robust, a new challenge emerged - difficulty swallowing. A terrifying incident that led to a diagnosis no one anticipated: stomach cancer.

At that time our focus in the School of Faith centred around the topic of healing, coinciding with the viewing of a compelling testimony video featuring a woman who experienced instantaneous healing from a stomach tumour. Being uplifted and excited prompted me to share it with my brother. He, too, watched the video and found encouragement in it. So began a time where he was receptive to receiving prayer during our weekly phone conversations.

The subsequent chapter of his story was surgery to remove the tumour and reconstruct much of his stomach, followed by a round of chemotherapy. A time of isolation, focussed effort at getting well again all the while upholding a positive outlook. A checkup revealed that he would need another round of chemotherapy. Things would be different this time, he did not want to face this alone. Packing up his flat, sending all his furniture and household effects to his young son and partner, to furnish their first home, he headed to Brisbane where he had arranged to have his treatment while residing with our sister and brother in law. It was a great comfort for him to be based there and have that support from our sis whom he adored. Halfway through the treatment, our sister's husband was diagnosed with a bowel tumour. This was such a difficult time for them all, but particularly for our sister, being torn between her commitment and love for our brother, and to be with her much-loved husband, as he embarked on his journey through surgery and subsequent treatment.

Once the chemotherapy was finished, my brother felt he could go back to Sydney to rebuild his strength and life again. Back on his bike riding every day, eating well, enjoying family and friends and radiating good health and wellbeing. In December of last year, he was given a full clearance from cancer. We were all so thrilled, so delighted he could start planning to make visits and take a holiday. In January one side of his face dropped. A visit to the doctor revealed he had what they believed was Bell's Palsy. This latest diagnosis was very difficult for him, not only as a very handsome man, the effect it had on his looks, but that his mouth had dropped, and he had difficulty keeping fluids in his mouth without needing a napkin to prevent spills. Now he was digging deep yet again to find the courage and strength to keep going. However, in late February, upon insistent requests for a scan, it was found that there were now tumours on the brain, in his cheek and spots of cancer on the spine.

In the dawning hours of a Melbourne morning where I was staying for an intensive weekend with the School of Faith, I received the news by way of a group sibling email. Immediately, I sought out some of our other New Zealand leaders who were slowly waking to the new day, asking them if they would join me in prayer for our brother? My arrangements to fly home were rescheduled to include a visit to Sydney to see him. Staying with his beautiful daughter in her apartment amongst the trees was such a welcome embrace for us both. So relieved was she to have one of her dad's sisters there to share in the unfolding shock and grief of the moment. Her explanation of the background and current situation was needed preparation to equip me prior to my seeing him in person the next day. The image of him cycling down the pathway to the wharf to meet me as I disembarked off the ferry in Rose Bay, has remained a vivid memory. Six foot five inches, tanned and oh so skinny. A man usually full of vitality and yet here he was incredibly thin, with hardly any energy. So depleted were his energy reserves he explained, that instead of taking me for coffee to his favourite cafe in the Rose Bay village, he could only manage the matter of steps across to the cafe in the park. After less than half an hour he apologised as he excused himself, he was too exhausted and needed to return home to rest. The next day we met again at the café by the wharf. However, this time he was able to cross the park to the benches only a few metres away, perfectly placed to encompass the stunning view of lake-like waters, little boats and yachts, waterside housing resting under a backdrop of encircling hills over the bay. As we sat under the canopy of the magnificent trees, shaded from the heat of the sun, I could see he was too exhausted for conversation, so we just sat. Some of the very few words spoken in that peaceful moment were in response to my tenderly rubbing his back. As he leaned forward, head down, allowing the comfort of the loving touch to act as a salve. "That is so good." Within twenty minutes his exhaustion levels had overcome him and he needed to return home. So weary, he needed to rest before the specialist appointment that afternoon. He very slowly walked with his bike beside me to the boat and as we neared the wharf where my boat would depart from, he stopped, turned his head towards me, looked me in the eyes and said, "I feel like I am fading away."

Grief filled tears were held back only long enough to allow him to depart, now flowing down my cheeks throughout the short clip across the bay into Sydney harbour by the Opera House. They continued to stream as I journeyed on the light rail through the city, passing Paddy's market to Piermont where my niece resides. They flowed as I prayed, worshipped and praised in the apartment, believing for the breakthrough to see him healed. A sacrifice of praise, in other words, praising when you don't feel like it. From February to April, three trips to Sydney including the funeral, my belief endured for a miracle! Regardless of the reality before me, my faith remains in a miracle-working God. I have seen with my own eyes, deaf ears opened, knees instantly healed, migraines depart, allergic conditions considered incurable - gone, a leg grow out a centimetre or two to line up with its mate, back realignment, to name a few, to know of His power to heal.

What is the purpose for my sharing this story of sadness, grief and loss? Because in hindsight, there were so many instances throughout this story where it would be so easy to lay blame. There were people responsible for what happened to my brother. If he hadn't been hit by a car where the shock and trauma may well have triggered cancer in his body? There were questions to be asked about why the doctor did not immediately send him for a scan when his face dropped? With his history, surely, it was important to check it out straight away? Would that have bought him more time or a different outcome? We don't know. There are moments here where it would be so easy to blame, easy to be discouraged. Easy to stay in that place of asking the questions "Why didn't they do this or that? Why did he not receive a miracle healing?" However, would staying in a place of blame, or disappointment have changed the outcome? Would our brother want us to be camped in these places? No, knowing his zest for life and intense love for his family he would want us all getting on with it and living our best life. His desire would be that we focus on the wonderful memories of fun times, laughter, music and being together. He loved all that.

Life happens to us all. Sometimes we are the cause and at other times we are the recipients of someone else's actions. There are scenarios where no one is at fault. In great grief and loss, it is important to take time to grieve and celebrate the wonderful memories. The key is not to hold onto blame but to look at how best to move forward. Depending on each individual situation where there could be a reason to blame, asking questions may be helpful. How did this happen, who was involved? How or what needs to happen to process through this? It is also a necessary step in the grieving process, as hard as this may seem, to consider the other person's situation or viewpoint. It might differ from ours but if we take time to intentionally listen, we may not agree but maybe we can understand, and in the understanding, we can forgive and no longer feel the need to blame.

Did discouragement set in when it seemed my prayers went unanswered? Never. I will persist in releasing healing and hold onto the belief in miracles. The passing of our brother will not be in vain. In fact it only intensifies the commitment. He will be celebrating in heaven knowing we keep on believing in the breakthrough.

> Take a moment to reflect in your journal. Write the word 'Blame' on the page. Now write down around the word anything that comes to mind where you feel you blame someone or maybe yourself for past events. If you feel there is still more needed here for you to be healed of self-blame, or blaming others, revisit the steps shared in the previous chapter on forgiveness and inner healing.

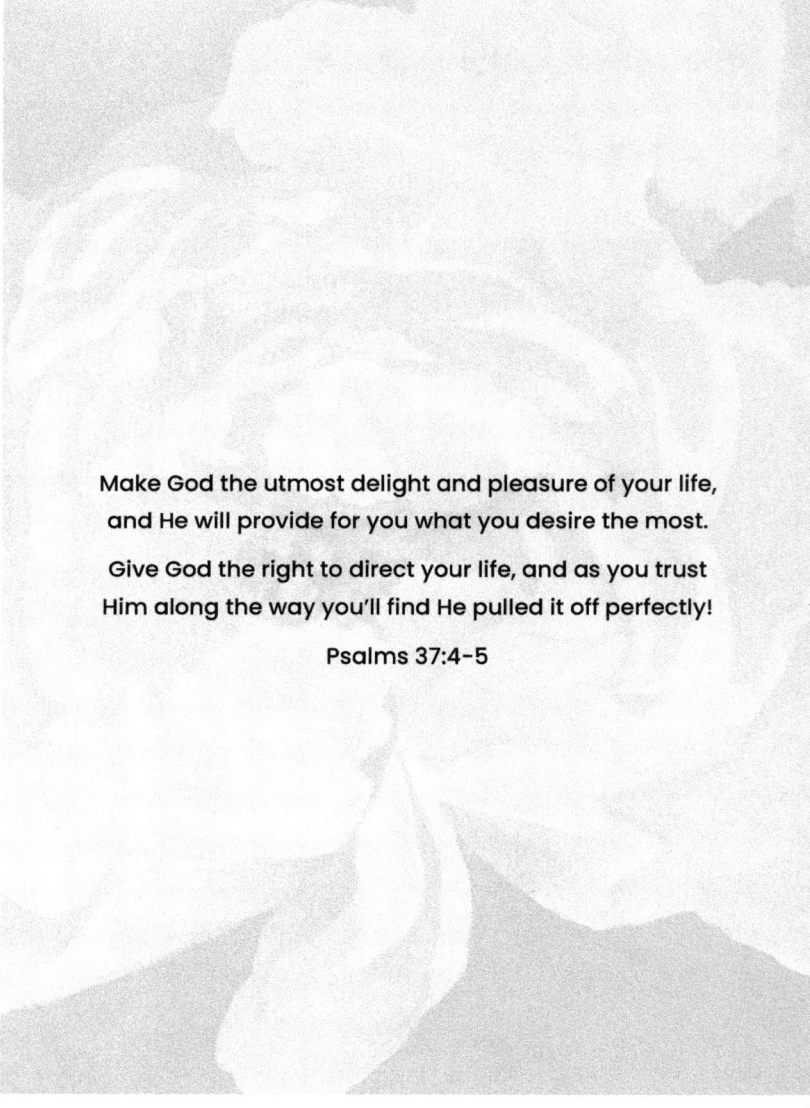

Make God the utmost delight and pleasure of your life, and He will provide for you what you desire the most.

Give God the right to direct your life, and as you trust Him along the way you'll find He pulled it off perfectly!

Psalms 37:4-5

CONCLUSION

Conclusion

Living on the bright side of life is possible in our world today. While it looks so negative at times, we can make choices and take actions that help us look through a different lens that is so much brighter.

The story shared in Chapter 12 was one I believed would remain untold. My husband and I had mutually agreed never to revisit it. However, our decision to be vulnerable and transparent now, is rooted in the desire to present a living testimony of how everything I have written about truly works.

Most of us can eventually forgive others. However, we can often find it difficult to forgive ourselves. Being called to bless the person who stole from us, I knew was possible. However, with the shame I felt over the scam, I was not sure I could forgive myself. To be able to tell the story, shows just how deep the healing has been. God has worked, not just in my heart, but in my husband's heart. He has brought us both through this painful journey of not only vowing never to speak of it again, but to be healed to the point of being able to share and to trust again. To walk on without needing to lay blame anywhere or on anyone. Look up and play You'll Never Walk Alone by Rogers and Hammerstein. Also popularised by Gerry and the Pacemakers.

We can rest in our storms, be filled with peace, regardless of what is going on around us. We can be positive in a negative environment by having hearts of thanksgiving and being grateful for the little things. We can walk in forgiveness of others and of self.

> **Be strong and courageous. Do not be afraid. Do not be discouraged or be in dread of them, for it is the Lord your God who goes with you wherever you go.**
> Joshua 1:9

The Lord our God goes with us wherever we go. He is our place of refuge. He is the answer to every question and the solution to every problem. He is our tranquil place, peace in the storm and our comforter. We do not face anything in our lives alone as He is ever present in us.

My prayer is that as you have reflected and journaled through these chapters and scriptures, you have experienced encounters of the Jesus kind. My earnest hope is that the outcome of this journey will empower you to now live on the bright side of life.

Acknowledgements

I wish to acknowledge Simon Fordyce, my proofreader and editor. Not only an experienced eye, but whose ability to suggest changes and point out corrections is professional, clear and direct, given with humour and encouragement. Working with you Simon was an absolute pleasure and delight. I highly recommend you to anyone who has written a book in need of your services.

Karen Pina, my coach. So professional and with the ability to keep our meetings sharp, on track and on point while still being warm, kind and sincere.

The creative team at self.publish.com. Thank you for the services you offer, the kind and caring team and for opening my eyes to a new way of getting this book out there.

Selwyn and Kelly Bennett, for taking the time, in the midst of a ridiculously busy schedule, to read the draft and write the Foreword. Thank you for your all-encompassing love and encouragement.

My husband Patrick, who regardless of the setbacks or disappointments, has always been my number one fan and advocate.

My three children whose love and support are such a blessing.

You, the reader. Thank you for picking up this book and making your way to the end. May your lives be richer for it.

The author and finisher of my faith – Jesus. For always being there, for keeping me in perfect peace in the middle of the storms of life. For filling my cup so full that it overflows with love and joy. For always believing that I will use the gifts you have given me for your Kingdom.

Author Biography

Bronwyn Hallot is a co-founder of Freedom and Life Church in the Wairarapa, under the Te Puna Wai Church Movement. She is a leader with the School of Faith, New Zealand. Her debut book <u>Is that You Papa? Tuning into the Voice of God</u> was published in 2021. A memoir style collection of stories which share the many ways she hears God's voice. Published as an encouragement to others to recognise when God is speaking to them.

Wife of Patrick, mother of three beautiful children, stepmother of two wonderful children, and grandmother of five very special grandchildren. Bronwyn delights in time spent with family and friends and being part of families of faith. Her passion to see people healed, transformed, restored to a full life in their communities because of an encounter with Jesus, is paramount.

Thank you dear reader,

Congratulations for progressing to the end. It warms my heart that you did so. I would love it if you would leave an honest review at bronwynhallotauthor@gmail.com

(Add Amazon link once created)

OTHER BOOKS BY THIS AUTHOR

Available on Amazon

www.ingramcontent.com/pod-product-compliance
Lightning Source LLC
Chambersburg PA
CBHW071303040426
42444CB00009B/1854